Camels

for

Uncle Sam

Camels
for
Uncle Sam

by Diane Yancey

 Hendrick-Long Publishing Co.

P. O. Box 25123   Dallas, Texas   75225

Library of Congress Cataloging-in-Publication Data

Yancey, Diane.
     Camels for Uncle Sam / Diane Yancey.
        p. cm.
     Includes bibliographical references.
     ISBN 0-937460-91-5
     1. United States. Army. Camel Corps—History—Juvenile literature. 2. United States. Army—
Transportation—History—19th century—Juvenile literature. 3. Pack transportation—Southwestern
States—History—19th century—Juvenile literature. 4. Camels—Southwestern States—History—19th
century—Juvenile literature.
[1. United States. Army. Camel Corps—History. 2. United States. Army—Transportation—History—
19th century. 3. Camels—Southwestern States—History—19th century.] I. Title.
UC350.Y93 1995
357'.043'0973—dc20
                                                                  95-6129
                                                                      CIP
                                                                       AC

Copyright © 1995 Diane Yancey

Design and Production
Intentions Graphic Design (Dallas, Texas)

Hendrick-Long Publishing Co.
Dallas, Texas 75225

TABLE OF CONTENTS

INTRODUCTION

The group of men and women paid little attention to the children playing around their feet or to the smells of cooking that drifted out of the town behind them. They chatted quietly, often glancing south, where the earth shimmered under the summer sun.

Suddenly, a small boy tugged at his father's hand and pointed. Shading his eyes, the man searched the landscape. Nothing moved. The horizon seemed empty except for a pale cloud in the distance.

The man squinted. The cloud grew larger, and now a faint tinkle of bells came to his ears. Behind him, people shuffled and murmured excitedly. The camels were coming.

Within minutes, several dusty, long-legged creatures came into view. Twenty-five in all, they moved across the ground with lazy strides. Neck bells tolled rhythmically as they swung past, taller than horses. The loads on their backs swayed from side to side.

A dog barked. One of the homely animals roared a rude reply. A baby began to cry.

Stone-faced, the turbaned drivers ignored the commotion and urged the camels forward. The crowd followed, eager to see what would happen next.

It was June 1856, five years before the first shots of the Civil War rang across America. The scene might have taken place in Arabia, but this crowd wore buckskin, and the camels were on American, not Middle Eastern, soil.

The caravan, the first of its kind, had just arrived by ship from Egypt and Turkey. It was under the protection of United States soldiers, passing through the frontier town of San Antonio.

Texas was about to come face to face with the United States Camel Corps.

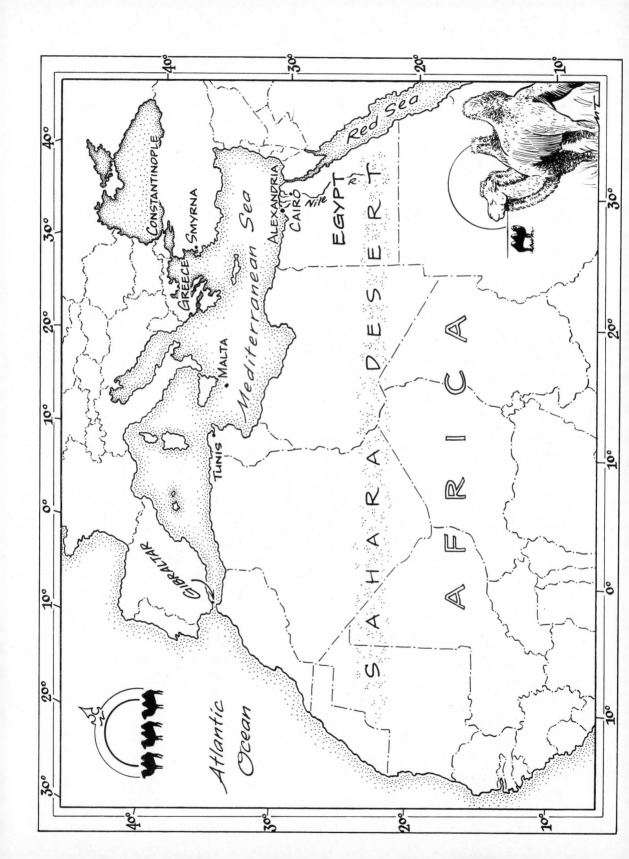

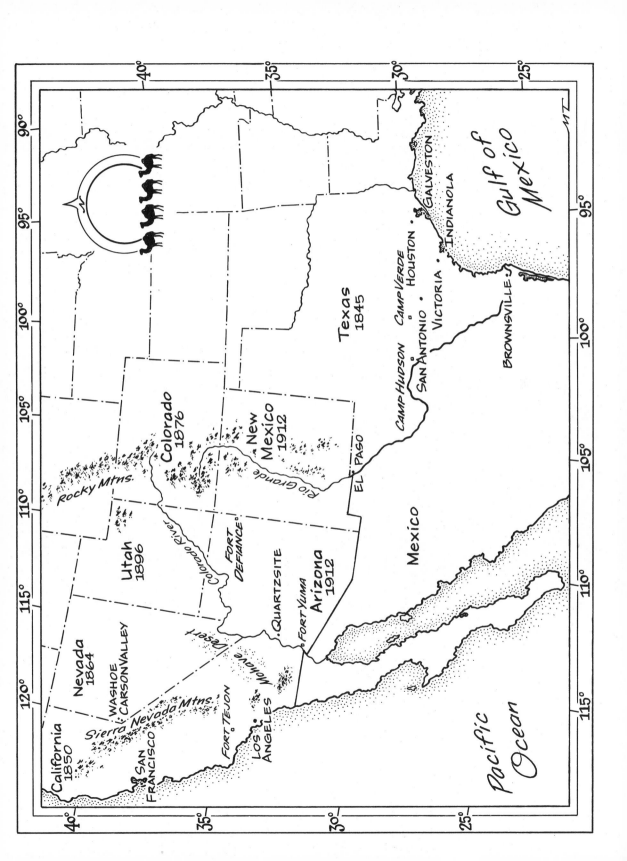

CHAPTER ONE

A Cargo of Camels

In 1851, Jefferson Davis, a tall, lean senator from Mississippi, stunned his fellow congressmen. He suggested that the American Army should enlarge its inventory of livestock to include — camels.

"For military purposes...it is believed the dromedary would supply a want now seriously felt in our service...," he stated.

As soon as they recovered from the shock, the congressmen

Jefferson Davis

laughed at the idea. Camels were creatures of the burning sands of Arabia and the Sahara, too rare even to be seen in American circuses or zoos. They were definitely not military equipment!

Senator Davis, future president of the Confederacy, ignored their scoffing. He calmly set forth the idea that Army Captain George Crosman had first proposed in 1837. Camels could be transported to the United States for use in the West. They were reportedly tireless, sure-footed, and able to survive in hot, dry climates. They would be perfect to use in exploring new territory, carrying supplies, perhaps even chasing hostile Indians.

Davis ended his appeal with the proposal that Congress bring a shipload of the animals to the United States for the Army to study.

In spite of their laughter, the congressmen had to listen. America had a transportation problem that needed a quick solution. With the opening of the frontier and the discovery of gold in California in 1848, thousands of settlers were moving west. There were few roads and no railroads connecting the two sections of the country. Delivery of mail and supplies was difficult and expensive. When danger threatened, the Army's pony soldiers had to ride long, hard miles to the rescue. Often they arrived too late to help.

The Army, like everyone else, used horses, mules, and oxen for transportation. These animals, while dependable in most cases, needed plenty of water, feed, and rest to stay fit for work. In the deserts of Texas and New Mexico Territory, where sunbaked grasses and dry water holes were everyday conditions, even the strongest suffered.

✛   ✛   ✛

As time passed, Davis was not the only one to support the camel project. Surveyors and soldiers who traveled in the West became convinced that the camel was the perfect answer to the country's frontier transportation woes. Westerners themselves seemed ready to give the animals a try.

"We might have an overland dromedary express that would bring us the New York news in fifteen to eighteen days...[but] we have not much faith that Congress will do anything in the matter," a Los Angeles newspaper editor wrote.

But Congress did do something. Four years later, when

Jefferson Davis again asked for camels, Congress not only

agreed, it set aside $30,000 (about $450,000 today) for the

project.

The first step was to purchase the camels. Davis, recently

appointed secretary of war, immediately sent letters to the men

he wanted to manage the project.

One went to a handsome

Army officer, Major Henry

Constantine Wayne. At Davis'

earlier request, Wayne had

read all available information

on camels. He believed

Henry C. Wayne

wholeheartedly in their fitness for use in America and agreed

to lead a camel-buying expedition to the

Middle East.

Davis also chose Lieutenant

David Dixon Porter to command

the *Supply*, a sailing ship that

would carry the camels back to the

United States. Porter, a naval officer

David Dixon Porter

who had gone to sea at the age of sixteen, had

twice served in the Mediterranean. He was no stranger to the

Middle East.

Gwynne (or Gwinn) Harris Heap, Porter's brother-in-law,

joined Wayne and Porter. Heap, a talented artist, volunteered

to record the trip by making sketches of the camels and their surroundings. Albert Ray, a muleteer (mule driver) and amateur veterinarian, was hired to help care for the animals once they boarded ship.

✛   ✛   ✛

The *Supply* left New York on June 3, 1855. By early August, Wayne and Porter had arrived at the port city of Tunis in Northern Africa, anxious to buy camels.

U.S.S. Supply

In the beginning, their eagerness overpowered their good judgment. They accepted the first animal offered. It turned out to be an ailing beast covered with sores and infected with mange, known as the "camel's itch." After much effort, and plenty of groaning and complaining from the camel, they managed to load the stubborn creature on board ship. Albert Ray got to work doctoring it with soapy water and sulfur ointment. Wayne and Porter set out again, vowing to make better purchases next time.

But good camels were surprisingly hard to find. Seven days later, with only three animals on board, they set sail for Malta (an island in the Mediterranean Sea), Greece and Turkey. There they had the same bad luck. In Constantinople, then the Turkish capital, Wayne learned the reason. War was being fought in the Crimea, an area north of Turkey. Most of the healthy camels were carrying troops and supplies in that war.

Drawing of an Arvana (single-humped) camel by G.H. Heap.

Still hopeful, the men sailed on to Egypt. They had purchased few camels, but they had seen dozens and felt like experts now. They knew that Arabian dromedaries, single-humped camels, were well suited for riding. The two-humped Bactrians, natives of central Asia, were used for carrying burdens. They knew that scarred animals

Drawing of a Bactrian camel by Heap.

had been sick or injured; a common native cure for any ailment was the application of a hot iron. They knew that a camel's

hump gave a clue to its health, and that underhanded traders

Embarkation of camels.

sometimes inserted a tube and blew air under the skin until the

hump looked firm.

In Egypt, Wayne found plenty of camels for sale, but laws

barred him from taking them out of the country. After applying for a special permit, he left with nine camels. He then sailed to Smyrna, now the Turkish port of Izmir, where Gwynne Heap had gone ahead.

After many more setbacks and endless wrangling, they finally managed to gather enough animals for a full load. Wayne paid an average of two hundred fifty dollars per camel. He also purchased several pack saddles and hired five Middle Easterners who agreed to care for the camels when they reached Texas.

With those details settled, preparations for the trip home went smoothly. The thirty-three grumbling camels and their caretakers settled into the barn Porter had built between the decks of the *Supply*. Only one hitch slowed the proceedings.

An enormous two-humped Bactrian — seven feet five inches high — was too tall to fit into its new stable. Porter directed that a hole be cut in the deck above so it could stand comfortably.

Although the camels were used to harsh treatment and poor living conditions, strict

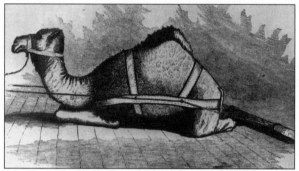

Heap pictures the camel tied to weather a storm at sea.

rules were set down for their care on the ship. They were cleaned, fed plenty of hay and oats, and watered daily. They were never left alone, and nothing was left in the stable that might cause them injury. Arabs and Turks thought nothing of beating the stubborn animals with sticks, but on board no one hit a camel with anything but the flat of the hand.

On February 15, 1856, the *Supply* set out for Texas on what proved to be a rough voyage. Almost immediately, violent storms arose. The camels had to be harnessed into a comfortable kneeling position to keep them from falling and hurting themselves.

The native camel drovers, even when they were not suffering from seasickness, paid little attention to the animals. Porter remarked in disgust that they "were so careless and so treacherous that something was wrong with their animals all the time...."

Fortunately, Albert Ray was qualified to take command of the stable. As one storm followed another, he had his hands full. Some of the camels refused to eat. Several pregnant females gave birth. Although Ray tenderly cared for the helpless babies, the stress of the voyage became too much. Only one, named Uncle Sam by the crew, survived.

Finally, after more than two grueling months at sea, the ship dropped anchor off the coast of Indianola, Texas, on the afternoon of April 29, 1856. Grunting and growling in typical

The Texas port of Indianola.

camel fashion, the awkward beasts were hoisted off the *Supply* and taken ashore.

The entire trip had taken almost a year, but Wayne counted it worthwhile. "I am happy to inform you that we have arrived, after an unusually rough passage, with one more camel than we started with," he rejoiced in a letter to Jefferson Davis.

Thirty-four camels were now safe on Texas soil. The experiment was well underway. Its success or failure depended on the next step — the ease with which the camels adjusted to life in America.

CHAPTER TWO

Nothing Runs Like a Camel

The camels' arrival in Texas made news across the country. No one, however, was happier on that occasion than the animals themselves. Feeling solid ground under their feet after months at sea, the beasts "became excited to an almost uncontrollable degree, rearing, kicking, crying out, breaking halters, tearing up pickets, and by other fantastic tricks demonstrating their enjoyment of the 'liberty of the soil.'"

The drovers managed to control the animals at last. Following Wayne's orders, they herded them into a corral outside of the nearby town of Indianola. There the camels settled, happily munching the fence made of rough prickly-pear cactus, popular with Texans because wood was scarce and because most animals avoided the plant's barbed thorns.

The camels stayed at Indianola for over two weeks, resting after their long voyage. Occasionally, Wayne used them to carry supplies from town. On one such day, he accompanied a camel and its drover on a trip to obtain hay.

A crowd collected when the animal appeared. Everyone watched with great interest as the beast knelt and the drover strapped two bales of hay, weighing over six hundred pounds, onto its back.

In response to its burden, the camel began to grunt and grumble. The onlookers murmured anxiously, certain that the beast would collapse under so much weight. Most mules could not carry half that amount.

Wayne directed the drover to strap on two more bales. The camel moaned pitifully, and the crowd began placing bets that it would never get up.

Then the drover tapped his animal. To everyone's astonishment, the beast easily got to its feet. Without seeming to notice its load, the camel lumbered away, the hay rocking gently from side to side.

✢   ✢   ✢

When the camels were fit for travel, Wayne set off for their permanent quarters at Camp Verde, an Army post sixty miles west of San Antonio. The trip took several days. One night the caravan camped near the small town of Victoria.

Most of the people living there turned out to see the strange animals. One of the families invited Wayne to dinner. The next morning, he thanked them by offering their ten-year-old daughter, Pauline, a ride on a camel.

"I was sitting high on the back of this unusual steed at whose head walked one of the Arabs, ever careful that no misfortune overcame me," she recalled.

Wayne also gave Pauline's mother a small gift of camel wool. The lady washed the wool many times to get rid of its unpleasant odor, then knit it into a pair of socks. They became a gift to President Franklin Pierce.

"If I had the machinery, I could have made you a better specimen of what the camel's wool could do in Texas," she

These camels are crossing a stream en route to West Texas.

assured him in a note accompanying her work.

✦ ✦ ✦

Even before Wayne had safely settled his charges at Camp Verde, he sent a letter to Jefferson Davis. The camels promised to be ideal in America, he wrote. They could be used for carrying supplies, messages, and soldiers. Perhaps, in times of war, small guns could be mounted on their humps.

For the present, however, Wayne proposed that the camels be given time to get used to their new land. During that time they should be encouraged to reproduce. A larger, stronger herd would then be available to meet the needs of the Army and the nation in the future.

Davis, who had already sent David Porter and Gwynne Heap on a second camel-buying expedition, disagreed. "The establishment of a breeding farm [does] not enter into the plans of the department. The object...is to ascertain whether the animal is adapted to the military service...."

Wayne submitted his proposal again, but with no success. His unhappiness with the project grew. So did his unpopularity among the enlisted men at the camp. They viewed Wayne as an outsider and resented it when he issued commands.

Finally, the major requested a transfer. As Porter, Heap, and the second load of camels arrived in Texas at the end of January 1857, Wayne left Camp Verde for good. Camp commander Innis Palmer and clerk Albert Ray were placed in charge of the camels.

Other leadership changes followed. In March, James Buchanan took office as the fifteenth president of the United States. Almost immediately, he replaced Jefferson Davis with a new secretary of war, John B. Floyd.

Secretary Floyd was as eager as Davis to make the Camel Corps a success. Congress had already set aside funds to build a wagon road from El Paso, Texas, to Fort Yuma on the Colorado River. Floyd assigned the Corps the task of surveying (describing and mapping) that unexplored territory.

Edward Fitzgerald Beale, a former Navy lieutenant who had explored the West with frontiersman Kit

Edward Fitzgerald Beale

Carson, was chosen to lead the expedition. Beale, a student of camel lore, had from the first encouraged Jefferson Davis to import them.

Enthusiastically, Beale put together his survey party. In addition to twenty-five camels, it included forty-four men, a dozen wagons, and a multitude of horses, mules, and dogs. At least two native drovers, George Caralambo (Greek George) and Hadji Ali (Hi Jolly), went along to help care for the camels.

The company set out on June 25, 1857. All remained alert

for Indian attacks, since the land they would be crossing was home to hostile tribes.

At first the camels seemed more of a bother than a benefit. After weeks of ease at Camp Verde, they tired easily. Each carried a fairly light load (for them) of less than six hundred pounds, yet arrived in camp hours after everyone else. Because

The Beale expedition. Painting by Narjot.

the size of their humps changed according to their condition, saddles needed constant adjustment. Until the soldiers learned the knack of packing, the camels suffered regularly from saddle sores.

Beale did not feel discouraged. He believed the camels would toughen up in time. "I see, so far, no reason to doubt the success of the experiment," he wrote in his journal on June 28.

He was right. Within a week, the camels were able to keep up with the wagons and mules. Sometimes they arrived first in camp after a long day on the trail. Beale was delighted by the beasts' stamina as they carried their heavy loads over the hot, rugged countryside. On steep, rocky slopes, they often led where mules refused to follow.

The company spent a few days at Fort Defiance in New

Mexico Territory, then officially began the survey, heading westward into unexplored regions. Now the camels carried heavy loads of corn needed to feed the mules and horses. Beale recorded in his journal that the camels themselves seemed to prefer eating plants no other animal would touch. They contentedly grazed on mesquite trees, greasewood, and screw bean plants that grew plentifully on the dry New Mexican landscape.

"Sometimes they bite off branches of considerable size and eat them leisurely, with apparent great ease. Their strength of jaw and teeth seems uncommonly great, greater even than in proportion to their size when compared with other brutes," Beale noted in admiration.

Long days of observing the camel in action gave Beale

time to appreciate the features that so well equipped it for desert life.

Long eyelashes protected its eyes from sand and sunlight. Its nose and ears could close tightly, again to keep out sand. Its feet were wide, with long toes and a tough sole, perfect for treading on sand or sharp rocks.

Blessed with four stomachs (the camel is a ruminant and chews its cud like a cow), the animal extracted every bit of nourishment from the bitter weeds and plants it enjoyed. During times of no food, it lived off the fat stored in its hump.

The camel normally drank as much as twenty to thirty gallons of water every three days. Beale and his men soon learned that it could go longer without.

By mid-September, hot weather and a lack of water had put

a strain on horses, mules and men. "…[W]e had watered our animals once with about four quarts each, and their distress was painful to witness," Beale wrote in his journal.

To make matters worse, the expedition lost its way. Only the camels seemed untroubled by thirst, so the seriously worried leader sent scouts mounted on dromedaries to look for a water hole.

Thirty-six hours later, the party's water supplies were exhausted. The situation looked desperate.

Horses eagerly drinking. Camels disdaining. Painting by Narjot.

Then the scouts returned to report that a river lay about twenty miles away across rough country. As the company stumbled to water, all had to admire the camels. They alone showed little interest in drinking.

"It is a remarkable thing how they stood it so well as they did, traveling under a hot sun all day and packing...[several] hundred pounds apiece," one of the men marveled.

✛   ✛   ✛

Almost a month later, Beale and his caravan came to the Colorado River. They had reached the western edge of the territory they had been sent to survey.

The expedition had seen plenty of Indians on its journey. Nervous soldiers had often spotted warriors watching the

Drawing by H.D. Bugbee.

camp at dusk. One evening, the men glimpsed ominous smoke signals rising above the nearby hills. Still, they were not attacked, probably due to the size and strength of their party.

In California, with the road survey completed, Beale split up the group. He headed south to Los Angeles with two of the camels. The rest were sent north to Fort Tejon. These animals were later moved to a camp in the Sierra Nevada Mountains to see how they would tolerate the cold. They spent the winter there and seemed to suffer no ill effects.

In February 1858, Beale left the camels in California. He headed east with his completed survey and a report on the animals in hand. Although he would not lead a camel expedition again, his journal summed up his feelings about the project:

> At times I have thought it impossible they could stand the test to which they have been put, but they seem to have risen equal to every trial....I believe at this time I may speak for every man in our party, when I say there is not one of them who would not prefer the most indifferent of our camels to four of our best mules.

The camels had proven that they could adjust to life in America. Leaders like Floyd, Beale, and Wayne became convinced that the beasts were the perfect answer to transportation problems in the Southwest.

Major General David E. Twiggs did not share their beliefs. Twiggs, who had assumed command of the Army in Texas in 1857, was an outspoken opponent of the project. Unfortunately for the camels, he was not alone in his feelings.

CHAPTER THREE

Does America Need Camels?

Major General Twiggs, a sixty-seven-year-old veteran of the War of 1812, was outraged when he discovered a herd of camels under his command. His reaction to the animals was simple. He hated them.

Like many Americans, Twiggs' dislike was based on ignorance and prejudice. "I know but little about the fitness of camels for the Army," he wrote to a fellow officer, "[but] I would not give one mule for five camels...."

In frequent letters to Secretary Floyd in the War Department, Twiggs used every argument he could think of to rid himself of the beasts. American soldiers preferred riding mules. The camel's worth was exaggerated; no animal could carry a six-hundred-pound load over miles of desert without faltering. The Texas command was too small to be "conducting experiments" with outlandish creatures from faraway lands.

Twiggs' letters always ended on the same note: "I do not want the camels in my command."

✛ ✛ ✛

Hatred of the camels was more than simple prejudice in many cases. Even the most loyal camel enthusiast had to admit that the animals had characteristics and habits that made them less than lovable.

The first, and perhaps most noticeable, was the camel's

distinct and disagreeable smell "more easily imagined than described." One traveler to the Middle East advised his readers to "pitch your tent as far from your camels as you dare, and, if there be a breeze, to the windward!"

Horses and mules reacted instantly to the odor. Whenever the camels came near towns or settlements, a rider went ahead, shouting, "Get out of the road, the camels are coming," in order to prevent a stampede. Farmers and muleteers all over the country soon developed a hatred for the beasts. City leaders in Brownsville, Texas, passed a law forbidding anyone to walk a camel through town because of the disruption it caused.

The camel's habit of spitting on anyone who angered it was more unpleasant than its smell. One muleteer remarked, "They were dirty things; they were nasty....[T]hey smelled bad and squirted dirt all over me." Soldiers considered the gluey, evil-smelling cud poisonous and believed it could cause sores if it touched their skin.

Camels were known for their bad tempers. Soldiers and muleteers had long been in the habit of beating mules to "get their attention." But when one soldier tried the same thing with his camel, the animal let out a roar and bit the man's arm, tearing the flesh from the bone.

Any wrong, large or small, was stored in the camel's cantankerous memory. It would take revenge when least expected, often by knocking down its "enemy," then crushing him with its heavy body. To sooth a vengeful beast, the drovers recommended placing an article of the offender's clothing in front of it. The animal would attack and trample the clothes for a time. When satisfied, its anger would be forgotten.

Aside from their personalities, camels were disliked for other reasons. Loading and unloading them was difficult. Americans had no experience packing goods around a saddle with a hole (and a hump) in the center. Worse yet, anyone who perched on a camel saddle and tried to ride one of the swaying beasts often suffered a severe attack of motion (sea) sickness.

✢ ✢ ✢

Although some disliked the camels, public enthusiasm spread as news of Beale's trip circulated around the country.

Otto Esche, a San Francisco merchant, was one of the most enthusiastic. He reasoned that camels would soon be much in demand to carry provisions to the gold fields in California. As

Descent to Carson Valley, Nevada. Painting by Edward Vischer.

a smart businessman, he wanted to have a supply of camels on hand.

In 1860, Esche set off on the first of three voyages he would make to the Orient. Over the next several years, he purchased ninety camels. All were two-humped Bactrians, preferred for carrying burdens. Only forty-five survived their sea voyage back to California, largely because of improper care and poor conditions on board the ship.

On his return to the United States, Esche sold the beasts to various businessmen who were anxious to take advantage of the animals' legendary strength and endur-ance. Several camels were taken to Nevada, where they were put to work packing heavy loads of salt to the Washoe silver

Drove of Bactrian camels on the way to the Washoe, Nevada, silver mills. Painting by Edward Vischer.

mills (salt was used in processing the silver ore).

Twenty-three of the beasts were taken to British Columbia, Canada, to work at a mining company there. Because of the rugged ground, the new owners equipped their animals with specially made leather shoes. When the camels did not live up to expectations, they were turned loose. Those that survived reportedly wandered south into Nevada and Idaho.

✛   ✛   ✛

Otto Esche was not the first private citizen to import camels. Two years earlier, in October 1858, a mysterious ship had anchored off the coast of Galveston, Texas. Its owner, Mrs. M.J. Watson of Houston, announced that eighty-nine camels were on board. She hoped to bring them into Texas to be used in place of mules and oxen.

Suspecting that the camels were only a cover-up for the lady's slave-smuggling activities, authorities refused to let the ship unload. When they found no evidence of illegal activity, however, they allowed the camels to enter the country.

By that time, Mrs. Watson had lost interest in the project.

The animals were set ashore where they wandered down the streets of Galveston, frightening horses and being attacked by rock-throwing youths. Frustrated town leaders soon passed a law stating "… no person or persons shall ride, drive, or introduce within the corporate limits of this city any camel or camels, except for the purpose of immediate shipment from the city."

Fines for breaking the law ranged from fifty to one hundred dollars.

The abandoned beasts were finally rounded up and taken to the ranch of F.R. Lubbock (later governor of Texas), who volunteered to care for them. People came from miles around to see the unusual animals. But Lubbock soon realized that the cost of caring for the camels could go on indefinitely. His goodwill faded. The Galveston incident ended with the camels being set free in the desert to fend for themselves.

✛   ✛   ✛

The Bactrian camel in California.

Meanwhile, the Army made little use of its two herds. A few of the California camels were used for surveys and for transporting goods in and around Los Angeles. Most of the Texas camels, stationed at Camp Verde, did nothing but eat, sleep, and reproduce. Captain Palmer, their caretaker since Henry Wayne's departure, relocated to Kansas in May 1858. (Albert Ray had left the camp in 1857.) The camels were placed under the "especial care and supervision" of Major D.H. Vinton, stationed in San Antonio.

Vinton had no great love for the animals, but he took his responsibilities seriously. In the spring of 1859, Secretary Floyd directed him to set up a camel expedition to explore the rough and rugged Texas southwest. Vinton obediently appointed Lieutenants William H. Echols and Edward L. Hartz as leaders. He also provided them with supplies and instructions needed to make the trip a success.

The expedition proved a brief but severe test of the camels' abilities. In late spring 1859, twenty-four camels, plus mules and drivers, set off from Camp Hudson in Texas bound west for the Rio Grande. Hartz followed Major Vinton's instructions and encouraged the camels to find food for themselves by gradually reducing their rations of grain. At the same time, the weight of their loads was slowly increased from four hundred to six hundred pounds.

Unlike Wayne and Beale, both Hartz and Echols held doubts about the camels in the beginning. By the end of the trip, each was a camel enthusiast. The camels had remained strong and healthy as the group journeyed across one hundred twenty miles of parched, rugged countryside. In addition, the beasts had carried enough water to supply the men and other animals. Without them, all might have died of thirst.

"The patience, endurance, and steadiness which characterize the performance of the camels during the march is beyond praise," Hartz wrote to his superiors.

✦   ✦   ✦

Secretary of War Floyd was delighted to hear that the camels had again demonstrated their worth in the American desert. To him, the animals were "a most useful and economical means of transportation for men and supplies through the great deserts and barren regions of our interior." He repeatedly suggested that government funds be set aside to purchase one thousand additional camels.

By late 1860, however, Floyd's focus had changed. His last report to Congress in December of that year did not mention the animals.

Floyd and other Washington officials were concerned with

larger issues now. The threat of civil war continued to grow.

No one's life would be untouched. That would be true for the

camels as well.

CHAPTER FOUR

Fate of the Camel Corps

By November 1860, tension over slavery and states' rights had risen to a fever pitch in the United States. Abraham Lincoln was elected president, although many Southern states had promised to leave the Union if that happened. They kept their promise. Shortly after Lincoln took office in March 1861, the Civil War began. Almost immediately, Texas joined the Confederacy. Rebel troops took over Camp Verde, including its more than fifty camels.

The Confederates made limited use of the imported animals under their care. As battles raged in the East, soldiers at

Camp Verde used a few of the camels to pack salt from Brownsville to San Antonio. The animals were also used to carry mail and to haul bales of cotton to Mexico.

Many Confederate soldiers hated the camels as much as their Union brothers had. One animal was pushed off a cliff that later became known as "Camel's Leap." J.W. Walker, a Texas Ranger, callously confessed to stabbing another:

> There was an old camel who would not keep up with the others; he always gave me trouble, and I hated the old beast. Well, this evening...he bit at me. I had a big dirk knife which I carried all the time. I just slipped up by the side of the old fellow and struck him...he died right there.

At the end of the war in 1865, Camp Verde and its sixty-six camels were reclaimed as federal property. With no real use for the beasts, the government put them up for sale. The highest bidder, offering only thirty-one dollars a head, was a Texan, Bethel Coopwood.

Coopwood, a former Confederate, already had fourteen former-government camels that he had captured during the war and taken to Mexico. With his enlarged herd, he tried to establish a freight service between Laredo, Texas, and Mexico City. That soon proved a failure. Coopwood recovered some of his losses by selling part of the herd to circuses and zoos. Other animals went to prospectors in Mexico and the Southwest.

Coopwood's ownership of the Texas camels ended soon after that. Unexpectedly, the government seized the rest of the herd, claiming them as stolen property. Coopwood fought the claim but did not win.

Ironically, the government soon rediscovered that the camels were more nuisance than benefit. Just a dozen years after being brought to America, they were released into the desert to make their way as best they could.

✛   ✛   ✛

The fate of the Army camels taken to California closely paralleled those in Texas. During the war years, the animals were well cared for but performed few useful services.

Because of that, in August 1863, a recommendation went to Washington from Lieutenant Colonel E.B. Babbitt, one of the officers responsible for the animals in California. "It is with reluctance that I have been induced to commend the public sale of the camels...," he wrote.

War-harassed officials in Washington agreed. In November of that year, the California herd went up for sale. Edward Beale purchased several animals. They lived out their lives in comfort on his ranch near Fort Tejon.

This photograph, taken about 1865, is the only known photograph of a camel in Southern California.

The rest were not as fortunate. Some went to zoos. Others were sold to tavern owners and confined in small backyard corrals to be viewed by curious customers. Thirty-six of the beasts were taken to San Francisco and sold at auction to Samuel McLeneghan (or McLaughlin), a California rancher.

McLeneghan planned to use the animals in Nevada for packing purposes. En route to that state, however, the rancher and his camels stopped in Sacramento where a state fair was in progress. Thinking to make a quick dollar, McLeneghan staged an impromptu camel race. He charged fifty cents per person and drew a record crowd.

The "Great Dromedary Race," as it was called, hardly lived up to its name. The camels seemed bored, refused to gallop, and had to be driven around the track. The race ended with the participants crossing the finish line in confusion, one man riding on a mule.

✛   ✛   ✛

When McLeneghan and his camels eventually reached Nevada, the animals were put to work under the harshest of conditions.

One professor from Yale University reported a distressing visit to the Washoe silver mills in 1865:

> *Their backs had not been cared for, and they had been used in packing heavy loads of salt from the deserts. Salt water and alkali had accumulated in the long hair of their humps, their pack saddles had galled them, and great loathsome sores nearly covered the parts touched by the saddle.*

Many of McLeneghan's camels, and others used to pack salt and freight, died after months of hard labor. Others suffered a fate similar to those in Texas. They were turned loose in the desert, often to be shot and killed by prospectors and Indians.

Camels in use in the Nevada silver mills.

Those that survived created such a nuisance to travelers that in 1875 the Nevada State legislature passed "An Act to prohibit camels and dromedaries from running at large on or about the public highways of the State of Nevada." The law remained in force until 1899.

+ + +

Four years after the war's end in May 1869, the transcontinental railroad was completed and linked the western United States with the East. That same year, the future Santa Fe Railroad, destined to stretch across the Southwest from Kansas to California, was begun.

The message was clear. With the coming of the industrial age, the government's need for camels had passed.

Its need for the native caretakers had ended as well. Left without work, some of the men returned to their homelands. Others remained in America. Of those who did, only the lives of a few were recorded in any detail.

Elias, a drover from Turkey, moved to Mexico in the 1860s.

President of Mexico Plutarcho Elias Calles, 1924 to 1928.

There he married a Yaqui Indian woman and took to ranching. One of his children, Plutarcho Elias Calles, grew up to become president of Mexico from 1924 to 1928.

Greek George stayed with the California herd when they were sold to Samuel McLeneghan and traveled with them to Nevada. After McLeneghan's death in 1865, George returned to California. There, he became a naturalized citizen in 1867. He took the name of George Allen, and settled down in a small adobe home in a part of Los Angeles that would become Hollywood. In his later years, he was described as "a modest, well-mannered, sturdy man, with a Homeric beard and a thatch of hair, both so dense as to seem bullet proof."

Greek George

Hi Jolly's life was more eventful. The stocky Syrian had developed "gold fever" on entering the United States. He divided his time between tending camels and trying to get to the California gold fields.

After the camels were sold, Hi Jolly married and became an American citizen, changing his name to Philip Tedro. For a time, he scouted for the Army. Then in 1889, to fulfill his dreams of finding riches, he deserted his wife and two daughters and began prospecting near Quartzsite, Arizona. According to some, he occasionally captured a camel and used it to carry supplies.

Hi Jolly later applied for an Army pension but was refused because he had never officially enlisted. He died, poverty-stricken, in 1902 and was buried in the tiny, barren Quartzsite cemetery. His gravestone, a small pyramid topped with a metal camel, remains a lonely monument to the camel project that once held so much promise.

Hi Jolly's monument in Quartzsite, Arizona.

CHAPTER FIVE

The Camel Tales

By 1868, the Camel Corps had vanished from the American scene. The camels had not. For years, they drifted over the desert, frightening settlers and spooking horses. One Nevada prospector rounded up a small band to carry his wares. In December 1881, Indians near Gila Bend, Arizona, captured several. Instead of following a usual custom of killing (and sometimes eating) the animals, the tribe sent them east to a circus in Kansas City.

As years passed, accounts of camel sightings in the Southwest grew into legends. Reports came from Texas,

Arizona, Nevada, Utah, and California. People repeated tales of a tattered old miner who led three camels laden with gold nuggets. Others claimed to have seen female camels with young; the sightings suggested that the herd continued to thrive in the wild.

One tale was told of a prospector who stumbled into an Arizona saloon on a hot afternoon. After quenching his thirst, the man worried aloud that his eyesight was failing. He swore he had seen a shaggy camel wandering on the desert.

An old man who stood nearby — the bartender called him Hi Jolly — looked interested when the camel was mentioned. Where exactly had the prospector seen that animal?

Getting an answer, Hi Jolly walked away without another word. Days later, he and the camel were found together in the desert. The old man lay with his arms wrapped around the neck of his shaggy friend. Both were dead.

Another well-known story was that of the "Red Ghost." This bizarre camel tale haunted the Southwest for almost ten years.

The legendary creature was first sighted in the spring of 1883. Two Arizona women and their children had been left alone on a lonely homestead while their husbands went hunting. While doing the morning chores, one of the women went to a nearby spring to get a bucket of water.

Suddenly, those inside the house heard the family dogs barking. Then came a terrible scream. Seconds later, something enormous and red rushed across the yard.

Terrified, the remaining woman locked the doors, gathered

the children around her, and waited. As dusk fell, she heard the welcome sounds of the men returning. Directed to the spring, they found the second woman's body trampled to death. A few long, red hairs hung from a nearby clump of willows. In the mud were mysterious hoofprints, twice the size of those of a horse.

A few nights later, two campers were awakened by a loud scream and a thunder of hooves. They stumbled out of their tent in time to see a huge four-legged creature disappearing into the darkness. Investigation the next morning turned up large hoofprints and red hairs caught on a bush.

Westerners were soon full of stories about the "Red Ghost." One man swore he had watched the mysterious beast kill and eat a grizzly bear. Others vowed they had seen it vanish into thin air. Cyrus Hamblin, an Arizona rancher known for his honesty and common sense, added a gruesome detail to his account. The creature carried something on its back. Hamblin swore that the "something" resembled a man.

Hamblin's solid reputation might have suffered if it had not been for another incident shortly thereafter. Five prospectors spotted an animal that they identified as a huge camel. The beast wore something on its back. When they tried to kill it, the camel ran for its life. Left behind in the dust was "a human skull with a few shreds of flesh and hair still clinging to it."

Faced with actual physical evidence, even the scoffers became convinced.

Stories about the Red Ghost multiplied, and nine years passed before the mysterious beast made its last appearance.

On that day, a rancher near Ore, Arizona, discovered an enormous red camel standing in his vegetable patch. The rancher snatched up his rifle. Carefully he aimed and fired. With one shot, the camel fell dead.

Those who examined the beast found no sign of a human body. However, as the *Mohave County Miner* reported on February 25, 1893, a strange patchwork of rawhide strips, wrapped tightly around the animal, confirmed that it had once carried a rider.

Who had been strapped to the camel's back? The placement of the knots proved that the victim had been tied on by someone else. Had he been dead or alive when lashed to the beast? Was the act murder or a cruel practical joke played against an innocent animal?

No one could say. The Red Ghost was no more. Its past was destined to remain a mystery.

✛ ✛ ✛

Today, many citizens of the Southwest believe that offspring of the first Army camels live, undisturbed by man, in the harsh landscape of Texas, Arizona, and New Mexico. Some even insist that they have seen the animals amble across the sands on quiet moonlit nights.

The legends may be only wishful thinking, but they point out a very real truth. In the words of one historian, "…it is romantic — and even comforting — to think that in remote areas of the desert Southwest there may be wild camels, descendants of those who originally wore the Army's 'U.S.' brand."

A unique chapter of American history is closed. The camels

who played a part in it will never be forgotten.

Mother camel and young. Drawing by G.H. Heap.

Notes

Chapter One

page 13   "For military purposes..."
Senator Jefferson Davis quoted in Harlan D. Fowler, *Camels to California*.
Stanford, California: Stanford University Press, 1950. 11.

page 16   "We might have an overland dromedary express..."
Fowler, *Camels to California*, 12.

page 22   They knew that a camel's hump gave a clue to its health ...
Odie B. Faulk, *The U.S. Camel Corps*. New York: Oxford University
Press, 1976. 53.

page 25   "...so careless and treacherous that something was wrong with their
animals..."
Lieutenant David Dixon Porter quoted in Fowler, *Camels to California*,
27.

page 27   "I am happy to inform you..."
Major Henry Wayne quoted in Faulk, *The U.S. Camel Corps*, 60.

C h a p t e r   T w o

page 29   "became excited to an almost uncontrollable degree…"
Lewis Burt Lesley, *Uncle Sam's Camels*. New Mexico: The Rio Grande
Press, Inc., 1929. 11.

page 30   On one such day, he accompanied a camel…
Fowler, *Camels to California*, 38.

page 32   "I was sitting high on the back of this unusual steed…"
Pauline Shirkey (Mrs. Robert Clark) quoted in Faulk, *The U.S. Camel
Corps*, 75.

page 32   "If I had the machinery…"
Mary A. Shirkey quoted in Faulk, *The U.S. Camel Corps*, 75.

page 34   "The establishment of a breeding farm…"
Jefferson Davis quoted in Fowler, *Camels to California*, 39.

page 38   "I see, so far, no reason to doubt…"
Major Henry Wayne quoted in Lesley, *Uncle Sam's Camels*, 147.

page 39   "Sometimes they bite off branches of considerable size…"
Lieutenant Edward Fitzgerald Beale quoted in Lesley, *Uncle Sam's
Camels*, 172.

page 40   "…[W]e had watered our animals once…"
Lieutenant Edward Fitzgerald Beale quoted in Lesley, *Uncle Sam's
Camels*, 229.

page 42   "It is a remarkable thing…"
May Humphreys Stacey quoted in Fowler, *Camels to California*, 59.

page 44   "At times I have thought…"
Lieutenant Edward Fitzgerald Beale quoted in Fowler, *Camels to California*, 62.

Chapter Three

page 47   "I know but little…"
Major General David E. Twiggs quoted in Faulk, *The U.S. Camel Corps*, 139.

page 48   "I do not want the camels…"
Major General David E. Twiggs quoted in Faulk, *The U.S. Camel Corps*, 142.

page 49   "…more easily imagined than described…" and "pitch your tent…"
Faulk, *The U.S. Camel Corps*, 70.

page 49   "Get out of the road…"
Chris Emmett, *Texas Camel Tales*. Austin, Texas: Steck-Vaughn, 1969. 30.

page 49   "They were dirty things…"
Ernest Moeller, muleteer, quoted in Emmett, *Texas Camel Tales*, 167.

page 50   The gluey, evil-smelling cud…
Faulk, The *U.S. Camel Corps*, 87.

page 50   But when one soldier tried the same thing…
Faulk, *The U.S. Camel Corps*, 87.

page 55   "…no person or persons shall ride, drive, or introduce…"
           Weekly Civilian & Gazette, Galveston, Texas,
           January 5, 1859. 1.

page 57   "especial care and supervision"
           Major D.H. Vinton quoted in Faulk, *The U.S. Camel Corps*, 122.

page 58   "The patience, endurance, and steadiness…"
           Lieutenant Edward L. Hartz quoted in Faulk, *The U.S. Camel Corps*, 187.

page 59   "a most useful and economical means of transportation…"
           Secretary of War John B. Floyd quoted in Faulk, *The U.S. Camel Corps*,
           152.

                              C h a p t e r   F o u r

page 62   One animal was pushed off a cliff that later became known as "Camel's
           Leap."
           Faulk, *The U.S. Camel Corps*, 156.

page 62   "There was an old camel…"
           J.W. Walker, Texas Ranger, quoted in Emmett, *Texas Camel Tales*, 161.

page 64   "It is with reluctance…"
           Lieutenant Colonel E.B. Babbitt quoted in Faulk, *The U.S. Camel Corps*,
           159.

page 66   The "Great Dromedary Race," as it was called…
           Fowler, *Camels to California*, 77.

page 67   "Their backs had not been cared for…"
Professor Brewer of Yale College quoted in Lesley, *Uncle Sam's Camels*,
127.

page 68   "An Act to prohibit camels…"
Lesley, *Uncle Sam's Camels*, 127.

page 71   "a modest, well-mannered, sturdy man…"
Charles F. Lummis, California historian, quoted in Faulk, *The U.S. Camel
Corps*, 170.

Chapter Five

page 74   One tale was told of a prospector…
Fowler, *Camels to California*, 87.

page 75   Another well-known story was that of the Red Ghost….
Robert Froman, "The Red Ghost," *American Heritage*. XII (April 1961):
98, and Faulk, *The U.S. Camel Corps*, 177.

page 77   "a human skull…"
Froman, *American Heritage*, 37.

page 79   "…it is romantic — and even comforting —"
Faulk, *The U.S. Camel Corps*, 190.

BIBLIOGRAPHY

"An Ordinance in Relation to the Introduction of Camels
Within the Limits of the City of Galveston," *Weekly
Civilian & Gazette*. Galveston, Texas, January 5, 1859.

Carroll, Charles C. *The Government's Importation of Camels:
A Historical Sketch*. Washington: Department of
Agriculture, Bureau of Animal Industry Circular No. 53, 1904.

Emmett, Chris. *Texas Camel Tales*. Austin, Texas: Steck-
Vaughn, 1969. San Antonio, Texas: Naylor, 1932.

Faulk, Odie B. *The U.S. Camel Corps*. New York: Oxford University Press, 1976.

Fowler, Harlan D. *Camels to California*. Stanford, California:
Stanford University Press, 1950.

Froman, Robert. "The Red Ghost," *American Heritage*. XII
(April 1961): 35-37, 94-98.

Ginsburgh, Robert. "The Camels are Coming!" *The American Legion Monthly*.
(June 1928): 12-13, 68-69, 71-73.

Gray, A.A. "Camels in California," *California Historical Society Quarterly*. IX
    (December 1930): 299-317.

"Jeff Davis' Dromedaries," *Time*. (December 8, 1930): 20.

Lesley, Lewis Burt. *Uncle Sam's Camels*. New Mexico: The Rio Grande Press,
    Inc., 1929. (Includes the report of Edward Fitzgerald Beale,
    1857-1858)

Illustrations courtesy of

Cover camel photo from *TEXAS HIGHWAYS* Magazine.

A B O U T   T H E   A U T H O R

Diane Yancey began writing for her own entertainment when she was thirteen, living in Grass Valley, California. Later she graduated from Augustana College in Illinois with a degree in biology. She now pursues a writing career in the Pacific Northwest, where she lives with her husband, two daughters, and two cats. Her interests include collecting old books, building miniature houses, and traveling.

"Almost all of the books I've written have some special significance to me. While writing *Desperadoes and Dynamite, Train Robbery in the United States*, I discovered that train robbers might have stolen gold that had been mined in my home town, located in the heart of California's Gold Country. My second book, *The Reunification of Germany* reminded me of my German heritage and gave me the chance to write about events surrounding a once-in-a-lifetime event, the fall of the Berlin Wall. *The Hunt for Hidden Killers*, a collection of ten medical mysteries, tied directly to my love of science. *Zoos* and *Camels for Uncle Sam* reflected my love and concern for animals.

"Even after working on a project for months, I find that the people and events I write about are still fascinating. If not for all the interesting stories waiting to be told, I'd be sorry to finish a manuscript and send it off to the publisher."

Ms. Yancey's books include *Desperadoes and Dynamite* (Franklin Watts), *The Hunt for Hidden Killers* (Millbrook Press), and *Zoos* (Lucent Press). In addition to *Camels for Uncle Sam*, a book entitled *Schools* (Lucent Press) will be published in 1995.